Steam Memories on Shed: 1950's – 1960's

No. 22: EASTERN REGION SHEDS
& THEIR MOTIVE POWER

Pictures by **K Pirt, D Beecroft & D Dalton**

Copyright Book Law Publications 2012
ISBN 978-1-907094-35-4

INTRODUCTION

This compilation of pictures illustrating the engine sheds within the Eastern Region of British Railways, along with their motive power, originates from the cameras of three photographers. Two of them, Don Beecroft and Keith Pirt play something of a supporting role in this album whilst the bulk of the views are the work of the late David Dalton.

From the early Fifties' until his death in 2009, David Dalton was well respected amongst the railway fraternity of Nottingham. Indeed, alongside his RCTS friends including Don Beecroft, John Hitchins and Don Boydon, he moved in the same circles as John Wilson and was photographing trains at Nottingham Victoria station at the same time as T.G.Hepburn. We owe a great debt of gratitude to these men for achieving, in photographic form, the memories which we now share, study and admire.

David was perhaps 'Champion of the Underdog' by which, for instance, he hunted down the last Horwich engine confined to its birth place, or loitered around Mansfield engine shed as the last of the Tilbury tanks embarked on their final trips. Likewise he searched out the classic 'Patriot' portrait taken on 13th November 1956 at Rugby; he had the knack of being in the right place, at the right time.

Some of his work shown here for the first time reveals something of the genius of the man devoted to steam and who still had the joy of a young 'spotter' etched into his face even in his latter years. His stories of railwaymen and engines could not be rivalled.

So, sit back and enjoy a trip around the engine sheds of the Eastern Region as they were in BR days; you don't even have to get off the coach.

Cover Picture B1 No.61208 outside Retford Thrumpton shed in February 1959. *K.R.Pirt.*

(previous page) Somewhere out in the Fens! Late 1950s! The coach has arrived at the western boundary of March engine shed, Norwood Drove. Already the notebook and pen/pencil brigade have dispersed around the site. There is a lot of ground to cover, its a big place and there are a lot of engines on shed, and we've still got five more sheds to do! The Sunday bash, a new depot, lots of lovely numbers. Some people embarked on longer expeditions from Friday night through to Sunday midnight! It was nice while it lasted and we still have the pictures along with the notebooks. Stored J17s Nos.65583 and 65576 met the crowds as they clambered down the path towards the shed but none of the hoard except a few would have given them a second glance. The pair appear to be in superb condition whilst the ground looks as though you could grow vegetables in it! *David Dalton.*

Printed and bound by The Amadeus Press, Cleckheaton, West Yorkshire
First published in the United Kingdom by Book Law Publications, 382 Carlton Hill, Nottingham, NG4 1JA

Annesley in 1959, with all the engines turned the correct way for their next duties! The 9Fs would be heading south to Woodford, as would the O1, whilst the B16 would be heading back to York on what was a daily working for these former North Eastern Railway locomotives. Soon the London Midland Region would come along and start radically altering the locomotive stock to the point where none of the classes illustrated would be allocated to this depot within a couple of years. A new Empire would come into being and like all historical events of such magnitude there would be casualties, waste and madness! *D.H.Beecroft.*

Before Ardsley shed became part of the North Eastern Region in July 1956, it was located firmly in Eastern Region territory, and coded 37A, with two other former Great Northern sheds beneath its wing – Copley Hill in Leeds (37B), and Hammerton Street in Bradford (37C). N1 No.69472 had spent its whole life in the West Riding working from either Copley Hill or Ardsley and in this Sunday morning view at the east end of the latter shed, it is ready for another week of duties hauling local passenger services. The date is 21st March 1954 and the 0-6-2T still has more than four years before withdrawal. Before that time however, No.69472 will receive a final General overhaul at Doncaster to keep it in fine fettle. *K.R.Pirt.*

Another Sunday at Ardsley, this time its 6th May 1962, with a semi-distinguished line-up of motive power comprising J39 No.64749, V2 No.60864, and A3 No.60092, complete with nameplate FAIRWAY. All were products of Gresley. Closure was still some time off – October 1965 – but none of this trio would see the ending for the shed. The Pacific, after arriving here from Holbeck (where it had worked over the S&C for a year) in June 1961, moved to more familiar territory at Gateshead in June 1963 but was condemned in October 1964. The V2 was a visitor from York where it was condemned in March 1964. The 0-6-0 was the least fortunate of the lot. Having arrived at Ardsley just after BR came into existence, the J39 did not survive until the end of 1962. *David Dalton.*

Barnsley engine shed had origins going back to 1845 but most of the structure being rebuilt here in late 1955 dates from a later period and was erected by the Manchester, Sheffield & Lincolnshire Railway with the Lancashire & Yorkshire Railway having access and regular use. With Barnsley (Exchange) station and the main line forming its western boundary, the two-road building, with its slightly larger yard, was never able to satisfy the stabling requirements of the resident engines so recourse to stabling them some distance away from the shed became normal practice at weekends. In this view we see an N5 0-6-2T and a couple of J11 0-6-0s but Barnsley also 'housed' eight-coupled freight engines for much of the LNER and BR periods; up to closure in 1960 some twenty or so 2-8-0s were allocated. After closure the shed was demolished to make way for a long overdue second platform at the passenger station. The yard was turned over to car parking whilst the level crossing which restricted movement at the southern end of the shed yard is still in business keeping the railway and road traffic apart. *David Dalton.*

The shed at Barnsley on Sunday 20th March 1955 before the builders got to work. This is the southern end of the building which shows once again the domination by former Great Central locomotives. Nearest is N5 No.69365 with J11 No.64343 behind; both Barnsley engines. The locomotive allocation at this time consisted about forty engines and most stabled on four sidings situated behind the photographer. To the extreme right of the picture is one of the skips associated with the small mechanical coaling plant, which was also on the right but out of frame. On the left is the less than inviting aspect of the single platform passenger station with its soot laden rear wall. Passenger comfort at the local stations had something of a low priority around these parts, coal was king as was reflected in the allocations of the motive power depots in the area, and Barnsley was no exception. *K.R.Pirt.*

Though coded 30C in the Eastern Region list, Bishops Stortford did not possess an engine shed as such and was simply a servicing and stabling point for locomotives, with a signing-on point for crews. However, at night and also weekends, a dozen or more engines could be stabled; at such times the goods yard on the Down side of the main line would be utilised alongside with the bay at the north end of the Down platform. The S.P. was located on the east side of the line – Up side – opposite the Down platform. A manual coaling stage along with a turntable completed the locomotive facilities whilst grounded coach bodies were used for offices and mess rooms. Prominent within the throng occupying the stabling roads throughout the Fifties were the N7s and Thompson L1 tanks but they were complemented by a couple of J17s throughout the decade. This view across the main line from the Down platform on Sunday 25th September 1955, reveals N7 No.69616 simmering between another classmate and an L1. By the end of November 1960 the stabling point had been abolished – 30C was no more! *K.R.Pirt.*

Cambridge shed, Wednesday 29th June 1955. D16/3 No.62567 straddles the ashpit as it goes through servicing. On the left a wooden bodied wagon sits in the sunken road installed during LNER days to assist in the removal of ashes although manual labour was still required to (a) lift the ash and clinker from the bottom of the ash pit to ground level and (b) shovel the mixture into the wagon! Once the fire, ashpan and smokebox have been cleaned, the 4-4-0 will reverse beneath the coaling plant; once the coal is loaded the tank was topped-up at one of the columns. Next, if necessary, it was onto the turntable, followed by a short trip to the shed for stabling to await the next duty. *K.R.Pirt.*

Cambridge and its still Wednesday 29th June 1955 as rebuilt J20 No.64683 simmers on the yard. The shed in the background managed to retain its northlight roof to the end, something of a feat regarding engine shed roofs. However, the covering on Cambridge's shed did not stem from the 1870s, 1880s, 1890s or even the 1900s! That particular structure was renewed in 1932 when the mechanical coaling plant was installed and other improvements carried out. The so-called 'wash-out shed' at March depot was also built at the same time when Government loans became the order of the day. In the event, the roof only lasted thirty years after all that because Cambridge engine shed was closed in the summer of 1962, demolished and turned into that favourite of us all – the car park! *K.R.Pirt.*

Part of the Sunday shift duties; getting locomotives ready for Monday's trains. This is Cambridge on 25th September 1955 with B2 No.61617 FORD CASTLE balanced nicely on the turntable. Considering so much money had been spent on Cambridge shed and its facilities during the 1930s, it seems surprising that nothing was left to provide for a vacuum tractor or electric motor for the turntable. Cambridge was a busy depot with a mainly tender engine allocation which required turning constantly. It was not unknown for Pacifics to turn up on King's Cross services, so when they did it was no doubt all hands. *K.R.Pirt.*

D16 No.62607 has gone through servicing and is now off to bed! *K.R.Pirt.*

The pride and joy of 31A – the immaculate B2 No.61671 ROYAL SOVEREIGN at Cambridge on Wednesday 25th September 1955. It had been nearly three months since this engine had returned from a 'General' at Stratford works but the paint shop finish was still apparent. In between its occasional 'official' duties, this B2 would ply the ECML route from Cambridge to King's Cross with one of the *CAMBRIDGE BUFFET CAR EXPRESS* workings. By October 1956 all ten of the B2 class were allocated to 31A, but their existence was tenuous and during 1958 and 1959 the whole class was condemned; ROYAL SOVEREIGN was one of the early casualties, being withdrawn in September 1958. *K.R.Pirt.*

Besides the Thompson rebuilds, Cambridge also had a number of the original B17s 'on the books' during the lifetime of the class. In BR days, No.61636 HARLAXTON MANOR was allocated to Cambridge from June 1950 to January 1952, then from the following February until June 1958. Here on 29th June 1955, it is looking as though it has just returned from a works visit but the opposite was the truth because it did not attend works until 25th August, and that for a 'General' at Doncaster. In the main, during the BR period, the B17s attended Doncaster for all their 'shopping' whereas the B2 class all went to Stratford for their repairs and overhauls. On the right is one of the LMR Stanier 'Moguls' which were regular visitors to Cambridge, and also to March. *K.R.Pirt.*

Out with the old, in with the new! Storage line Cambridge shed, 23rd August 1953. Throughout the LNER period new locomotives were introduced to replace the pr-Grouping types and the process continued into BR days. However, many of those ancient locomotives were kept going – stored with a view to using them at some point – the two E4s nearest, Nos.62786 and 62781 lasting into 1956. *David Dalton.*

Cambridge, 23rd August 1953, a perusal of the storage line reveals F6 No.67221, and E4 No.62790, the latter with a tender full of coal and no chimney covering. The 2-4-2T was in and out of storage here and was transferred to King's Lynn in September 1954 only to return in December whereby another stint in storage took place until a transfer to Stratford was arranged in December 1955. The days of the 2-4-2T classes were numbered and No.67221 was condemned in October 1957 and by the following May Class F6 became extinct. The E4 was soon out of its temporary unemployment because in September it was chosen to work the R.C.T.S *East Anglian Special* from Cambridge to Liverpool Street via Hitchin and Palace Gates. Two more years of work at Cambridge; shed pilots, pick-up goods, passenger services to Colchester, etc., became its lot before withdrawal in January 1956. *David Dalton.*

The east end of Colchester shed in 1959, looking towards the station. The electrification catenary is up and ready to feed the new motive power, so the days of Colchester shed – 30E – are numbered. By the middle of December the remaining steam locomotives will have been either withdrawn or dispersed to other sheds. At the beginning of the year some fifty-five engines resided here and 80% of those were tender engines. Goodness knows how the place managed but manage they did. Witness the discarded leaf springs tossed on the scrap pile to the right - a local repair carried out under less than ideal conditions. J15 No.65446 stands over an inspection pit and may well have been the recipient of new springs because it survived the December closure and moved on to Stratford shed for another twelve months of work before being withdrawn in December 1960, aged 61 years! Nine other J15s were resident here in January 1959 and of those only four moved onto pastures anew. Perhaps the biggest impact was made on the five resident B17s, two of which were condemned just before the shed closed; the others transferred to Stratford too but were withdrawn during the first weeks of 1960. Their days as a class were numbered anyway but the sudden and radical change at Colchester was something that was taking place all over the country and would continue to occur until steam was finally eradicated some nine years hence. The shed here dated from 1890, built by the GER, it had a roof of the northlight pattern which had to be replaced in 1936 by a conventional pitched style but with stepped gables as in the illustration. The first shed provided for the engines at Colchester was erected in 1843 by the Eastern Counties Railway. That did not last long and was replaced in 1846 by one built for the Eastern Union Railway but that was burnt down in 1850. Yet another shed was erected by the EUR which, with a later extension, lasted until replaced by the Great Eastern building. *David Dalton.*

Much, but not all, of Colwick shed is illustrated in this view captured on Friday 17th July 1964. On the left is the lofty, two-road repair shop. To the left of that building, out of sight, is the original four-road shed of 1876 which was the nucleus of this once great depot. Coming back to what is on show we have, next to the repair shop, the eight-road shed dating from 1882 but which had been re-roofed by BR. Finally, on the right and accommodating wagons on some of its four roads, was the shed commissioned in 1897 to house thirty-six locomotives but was by now given over to wagon repair. Alongside that, and out of picture, was a two-road, purpose built wagon shop which came into use at the same time as the four-road building. The locomotives on show certainly reflect the Colwick allocation at this period with remnants of the old LNER regime represented by the Thompson B1s, and the lone WD 2-8-0 beyond the two nearest B1s. Representing the new LMR regime are the two Ivatt Class 4s, the vanguard of what was about to descend on Colwick in the shape of Stanier 8F and Class 5s. On the road leading to the fitting shop are some of the depot's handful of diesel shunters which were housed in the shop in an attempt to keep their delicate innards being polluted by the contents of the steam shed. Modellers note the three sets of locomotive wheels sat on the ground between the two factions. The history of Colwick was reflected in the fortunes of the Nottinghamshire and Derbyshire coalfield which rose to prominence in the 1890s but went into decline during the 1960s and was left with a few super pits open until the 1990s, served by the railways once belonging to the predecessors of the LMR. Colwick closed its doors at the end of 1966, some ninety years of history coming to a close. *David Dalton.*

Colwick in the happier days of March 1956 with one of the depot's own K3s, No.61821, in the main yard. Go to this location now and not a trace of this once great engine shed remains. It was the largest of the Great Northern sheds and could rival many other places too. The original northlight roof of this shed – big shed – required renewal by the time of Nationalisation and BR eventually rebuilt the roof using lightweight framing and 'Patent' glazing; the gloom of the interior brings the truth of the last mentioned material into question. *K.R.Pirt.*

B1 No.61183 bathes in the morning sun at the south-east corner of Sheffield Darnall shed on Sunday 6th February 1955. Except for the first couple of weeks of its life spent running-in from Gorton shed (most of the Vulcan Foundry built B1s went initially to Gorton for acceptance and running-in), this engine worked thereafter solely from Darnall until withdrawn in July 1962. This view shows the engine just a couple of months out from a General overhaul at Darlington works hence the relative cleanliness. On the right are the roller-shutter doors of the two-road repair shop, a facility incorporated into the shed building when Darnall was built during WW2; the high pitched roof discernible on the left topped a 100,000 gallon water tank which was also incorporated into the structure of the shed. *K.R.Pirt.*

This aspect of the western end of Darnall's considerable yard shows a number of K2s stored for the winter. Although not the best of illustrations, it was after all a murky 18th December 1955 in Sheffield, we get to see the locomotive storage ground from a different viewpoint; the elevated road in the background was the normal camera position. Keith Pirt listed the nine 2-6-0s which were spending winter here as Nos.61724, 61728, 61737, 61739, 61747, 61749, 61759, 61760, and 61761. All were recent – June 1955 – additions to Darnall's allocation with Nos.61724 and 61739 arriving from Immingham, Nos.61728, 61760 and 61761 coming from Boston, whilst Nos.61737, 61747, 61749 and 61759 were all ex Colwick. Of course all of them went back to work in the spring of 1956, some from Darnall shed, with a few transferring back from whence they came. Note the piles of coal alongside the tenders; the corrosive effect of wet coal on sheet steel was legendary hence the necessary labour-intensive activity required to empty the tenders. Note also the paint jobs on the smokebox area, another part of the locomotive which might succumb to corrosion unless protected; the usual chimney protection is also in evidence. *K.R.Pirt.*

It wasn't very often that you spotted a clean Gateshead Pacific so relish this view of Peppercorn A2 No.60538 VELOCITY at Doncaster shed on Sunday 6th December 1953. Of course, this A2 is ex works after a 'General' (5th November to 4th December 1953). No.60538 was one of the five fitted in 1949 with the multi-valve regulator, which, with its associated rodding is prominent and therefore somewhat spoilt the appearance of the engine. *K.R.Pirt.*

Doncaster shed, July 1951, with brand new, just out of the box Ivatt Cl.4s Nos.43138 and 43139 stabled in the usual place for ex works locomotives, adjacent to the coaling plant. No.43138 (Works No.2083) was the second engine of Lot 1308, Doncaster's penultimate batch of these 2-6-0s which they were building for all and sundry. As can be seen, this engine was destined to start work at 65A Eastfield, whilst No.43139 would probably accompany it as far as Gateshead, at which point the latter engine would head west over the Pennines to Carlisle Canal shed. A few days running-in around Doncaster – trips to either Sheffield, Retford and Scunthorpe would be the norm – prior to working north up the ECML to Edinburgh then across to Glasgow. How long that particular journey would take depended on the depots' playing host during the Class 4's passage. Some places tended to use migrating locomotives for a couple of days or more prior to releasing them to continue onwards, others simply coaled and watered them before sending them on their way. For the record, No.43138 spent the next ten years working at various sheds in Scotland prior to transferring to the NER where, in March 1967, it was withdrawn at North Blyth. On arrival in Carlisle, No.43139 liked it so much that she decided to stay to the end and only moved from Canal to Kingmoor on closure of the former shed. Withdrawal took place in September 1967. The bulk of an LNER Pacific tender protrudes on the right; this one belonged to A4 No.60026 MILES BEEVOR. *K.R.Pirt.*

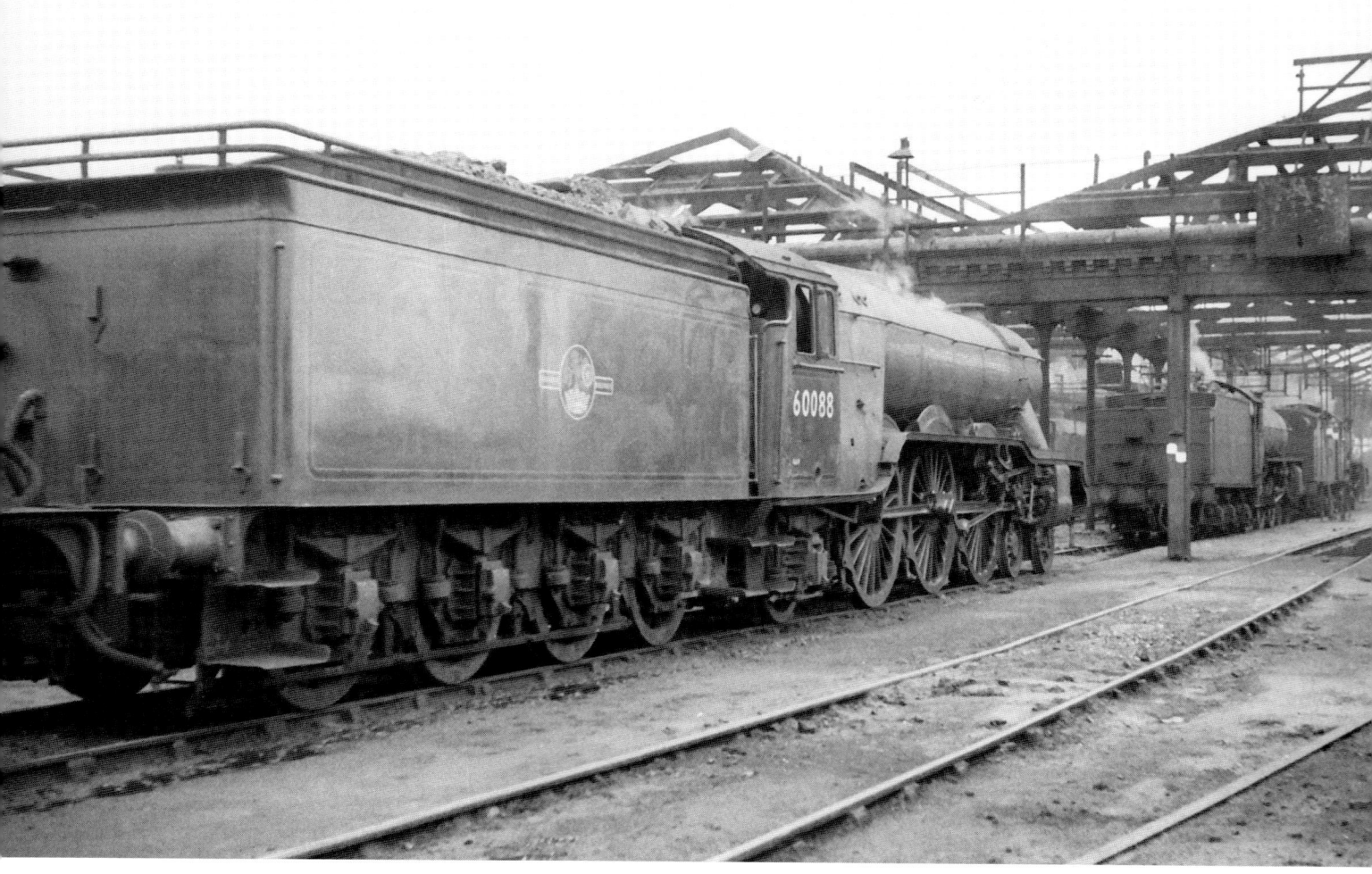

A nice three-quarter rear view of Heaton based A3 No.60088 BOOK LAW outside the temporarily de-roofed Doncaster shed in July 1958. The shed was undergoing rebuilding under a scheme started during the previous year and still had some way to gone for completion. During the rebuild, opportunity was taken to create a 'clean' area for the forthcoming diesel fleet and No.10 road was removed so that a steel framed, asbestos clad, wall could be erected over the filled-in pit. Nos.11 and 12 roads (on the east side of the shed) then became steam locomotive maintenance roads until the advent of the diesels. Note the wrong facing BR crest on the Pacific's tender; that was applied during a 'General' in September 1957 ad would be corrected during a visit to works in 1958. *D.H.Beecroft.*

A look across the yard at the north end of Doncaster shed in August 1958 with a cosmopolitan throng of locomotives from various origins: Great Eastern, War Department, Great Central, Great Northern, London Midland & Scottish, and LNER. Such was the draw of Doncaster for enthusiasts. Fifty years beforehand it would have been the same at this place with engines from the North Eastern, Great Central, Great Eastern, Lancashire & Yorkshire, London & North Western, Great Northern of course, and possibly the WD or ROD as it was known then. The J68 was part of 36A's allocation, one of a dozen ex-GER 0-6-0Ts on the depot's books at that time. Note that there is not a Pacific in sight! *D.H.Beecroft.*

Now then, who was responsible for fitting these smoke deflectors to A3 No.60097 HUMORIST? Whoever it was certainly had a sense of humour or total contempt for one of Gresley's masterpieces. Luckily for enthusiasts based in England, this Edinburgh based engine rarely appeared south of Newcastle during BR days and only visits to the works at Doncaster brought it further south. This visit, for a General overhaul which concluded in February 1962, was to be its last major repair and No.60097 returned north to St Margarets shed; during its absence it had been reallocated to 64A in the previous December so that 64B Haymarket shedplate will have to be removed. Those smoke deflectors were fitted in April 1947 as an ongoing experiment to rid the class of smoke problems experienced at speed, mainly by engines equipped with Kylchap double blastpipes. The similarity of the deflectors to those fitted to the Peppercorn Pacifics is more than a coincidence. The date of this picture is Saturday 10th February 1962, just prior to the running-in routine which the A3 would start on Monday next. *K.R.Pirt.*

Doncaster shed, Sunday 15th March 1959, with another Gateshead charge in ex-works condition. A3 No.60091 CAPTAIN CUTTLE had just finished a 'General' and had been brought on shed the previous day ready to start the running-in routine. Note the high position of the shedplate on the smokebox door. *D.H.Beecroft.*

Doncaster shed outlet in June 1962 with Peppercorn A1 No.60128 BONGRACE waiting for the signal to reverse down to the station to take on a southbound working. A resident of 36A since April 1959, this A1 would end its short life here in January 1965 as Doncaster shed became virtually the last bastion of main line steam on the old Eastern Region. *K.R.Pirt.*

Enfield on Wednesday 25th May 1960 with N7s Nos.69687 and 69729 stabled outside the single road engine shed. This is the year when electrification came to Enfield and the work of these 0-6-2T would be drastically curtailed and both were condemned four days after the shed here was closed. A sub shed of Stratford, and built by the Great Eastern in 1869, the shed was closed on the last day of November 1960. *David Dalton.*

Before the catenary arrived! Enfield engine shed as seen from the platform at Enfield (Town) station, on Sunday 31st May 1959, with N7 No.69658 stabling for the weekend. The length of this single road building, which dated from 1869, can be appreciated from this angle. *David Dalton.*

N7 No.69663 has its tanks topped-up at Enfield on 30th May 1960 whilst electrification work continues above. The proximity of the catenary post to the water column is interesting and raises the question 'was it set further back from the rails so that the column was not disturbed?' Certainly, at this stage of the scheme, it was not worth the expenditure to re-site the water mains and it was deemed acceptable to increase the span of the catenary by a few more feet. Note the man working on the wiring above the mineral wagon! Where's the H&SE chap then? *David Dalton.*

Photographic evidence over a period of years shows that all five of the push-pull fitted F5 used on the Epping-Ongar shuttle services in the 1950s, Nos.67193, 67200, 67202, 67203 and 67212, were all in a deplorable external condition, especially around the front end. This view of Epping shed yard on Sunday afternoon, 28th April 1957, with Nos.67193 and 67200, stabled outside the shed, supports those observations. Within six months these engines would be made redundant when the London Underground extended their services to Ongar in November. The turntable visible on the left of the illustration was used to turn the goods engine which visited the Loughton branch each day. *David Dalton.*

Hardly the image to gain public confidence! Nos.67193 and 67200 show their flanks to the setting sun at Epping. The shed here had been rebuilt by London Transport in 1949 as part of the agreement that BR would provide the motive power for the shuttle service to Ongar. *David Dalton.*

The unmistakable concrete structure of Frodingham engine shed gives away the location of this J39 on Sunday 10th October 1954. The meaning of the chalked cross and adjacent markings on the cabside is unknown but the small figures of the 64831 number tells us that this Ardsley based engine was one of the many Eastern Region engines which visited the LMR works at Derby for a General overhaul. Of course, that was back in January and February 1952 and the 0-6-0 is ready for another boiler change. That took place some five weeks later when No.64831 attended Gorton works for a 'General' (13th November to 24th December 1954), its penultimate heavy overhaul. Note: not only is the weather clear and bright, the atmosphere around the depot appears to be somewhat brighter than usual, as though the nearby steel plants have shut down which of course they hadn't. *K.R.Pirt.*

Only thirteen Q1 tank engines were ever created from rebuilt Q4 0-8-0 tender engines. The initial order for the rebuilding programme encompassed twenty-five engines but in the event we had to make do with that 'unlucky for some' or 'bakers dozen' depending on how you view them. From their introduction in mid-1942, Frodingham shed was to play home at one time or another to ten members of the class and here in late 1958, No. 69936 shows off its deplorable external condition. Built for heavy shunting duties the class was scattered all over the northern half of the former LNER system with a couple resident at Eastfield. Most ended their days at Frodingham as did No.69936 in September 1959, when it became the last of the class. *David Dalton.*

Grantham during its final days as a motive power change-over point. Mimicking thousands which had gone before it, A3 No.60047 DONOVAN creates a smoke nuisance whilst waiting to go off shed in June 1961 to handle a northbound working. Shortly after this date the A3 was fitted with the trough-like smoke deflectors which had been proven, on those engines equipped with double chimneys, to lift the smoke clear of the cab whilst at speed; the fitting was carried out at King's Cross shed as this engine had completed a 'General' overhaul just three months previously and would not have been scheduled to attend worked again for some time. The worksplates were repositioned on the cabside at the same time, below the number, a pleasing conclusion in the event. *K.R.Pirt.*

King's Cross A4 No.60029 WOODCOCK is about to use the unique Grantham scissors triangle in order to be headed in the right direction for working home in May 1960. With the late afternoon sun highlighting their magnificent steed, the crew pose at Keith Pirt's request before going about the operation. This A4 had been fitted with a speed indicator during its last 'General' in March. The tenders in the left background, one still marked NE, were used as sludge carriers for emptying the contents of the water softening plants, one of which had been built at Grantham shed. *K.R.Pirt.*

What to do with surplus motive power for which no suitable traffic is available anyway? Such were the dilemmas facing the authorities on BR in the early Sixties' as more and more well maintained and perfectly serviceable steam locomotives became surplus. N2 No.69568 had, up to late May 1962, been part of the King's Cross stud of 0-6-2Ts working the suburban services in and around the London terminus. However, diesels had taken over, the N2 was transferred to New England, and that depot was struggling to find a use for it. Sent to Grantham, it was photographed alongside the west wall of the 'new' shed at that place in August 1962. The engine appears out of use but Grantham had, for some years now, been using N2s for station pilot duties. Whatever employment No.69568 found, it did not last for long as it was condemned the following month but took another six before being accepted into Doncaster 'Plant' works for cutting up. *K.R.Pirt.*

With three more of its ilk within touching distance, King's Cross A3 No.60059 TRACERY poses for this near-broadside view whilst stabled on Grantham's yard on a Sunday afternoon in June 1961. For enthusiasts, and photographers alike, one of the attractions of Grantham shed was the constant coming and going of express passenger engines from the length and breadth of the ECML More often than not King's Cross A3s would work an express to Grantham, be relieved by another Pacific from either Newcastle, Leeds, Doncaster or York, visit the shed for servicing ready for return to the capital with another express. That express would have been brought south by any one of the Pacifics allocated to sheds in faraway places. They in turn would come on shed for servicing and turning ready to work the next northbound express which required fresh motive power. It was an on-going operation, 24-hours a day, 364 days a year – December 25th was regarded as a holiday, even then. Such was the intensity and the complexity of the constant traffic that it seemed that it would last forever! *K.R.Pirt.*

Hornsey shed, November 1955, with No.69567, 69533 and a visiting 9F in view. The coaling plant lends some substantial background to the picture along with the ever changing haze of smoke and steam. Besides its small army of 0-6-2T, Hornsey had a substantial allocation of 0-6-0 tank engines for working the local yards and for moving trains from those places to various locations around London, including yards on both the Southern Region and the Western Region. The shed rarely possessed more than a handful of tender engines and those were inevitably 0-6-0s to work the pick-up goods between north London as far as Hitchin. Many of the large freight locomotives working into the area from the north were serviced at Ferme Park prior to returning whilst some, as witness the 2-10-0 on the left, visited the engine shed at Hornsey for coaling, etc. *K.R.Pirt.*

During the early years of the Fifties, Ipswich engine shed underwent a complete modernisation. Its ancient dilapidated accommodation was torn down, the yard layout was remodelled to allow easier movement and egress, a mechanical coaling plant was erected and a new prefabricated concrete building was created to house the ninety or so steam locomotives allocated to 32B. The new shed spanned six roads, four for everyday servicing, which had ventilators in the roof, and two other roads for heavier maintenance which were partitioned off and had pits with the luxury of built-in lighting. Doors were provided at each end of this section but roof ventilators were absent, the idea being that locomotives would be 'dead' when pushed into this 'clean' shed for examination, repairs, etc. Someone, even as far back as 1950 when the plans were finalised but steam was still king, probably had the idea that diesels might one day use the shed. Even so, the ideal modernisation of steam depots and the provision of accommodation for diesels was not that far apart anyway because both had frailties which required looking after. This is the southern aspect of Ipswich shed on Sunday 23rd August 1953, shortly after rebuilding was completed. *David Dalton.*

The northern end of Ipswich on the same Sunday in 1953, with J15 No.65361 prominent amongst the throng of mainly LNER Standard locomotives. Note that the two roads outside the 'clean' shed stable engines which are in steam. To enact the ideal situation for locomotive maintenance required disciplines and procedures which had not yet been learnt. Diesels did eventually take over at Ipswich but their inheritance did not last long after steam was evicted. *David Dalton.*

The eastern end of King's Lynn engine shed on the morning of Sunday 1st February 1959. This four-road structure was another which had survived the ravages of time without any major maintenance being carried out since it was built by the Great Eastern in 1871. The site on which it was located, just outside the eastern end of the passenger station, became cramped and was hemmed in by the lines serving the goods depot and docks branch. BR (ER) wanted to dieselise this area of the region as quickly as possible and places like King's Lynn became prime targets for closure to steam, an event which took place on 12th April 1959, just ten weeks after this scene was recorded. Note the dog-leg in the south wall of the shed, evidence perhaps that even as it was being built the site was restricted. Although open at both ends, each with four openings to allow through running and more flexibility, the southernmost road – identified by the tarpaulin draped across the entrance – never was connected to the other roads at this end of the shed yard. Although this shed could boast an allocation nearing fifty locomotives at the end of the LNER, less than twenty were present when the plug was pulled in 1959. The diesels duly took over the building but only for a year or so until a new one-road diesel servicing shed was brought into use and this edifice of the steam age was demolished. Note the Brush Type 2 lurking in the distance. *David Dalton.*

43

Forlorn, unwanted, unkempt. This J69 had little going for it when photographed after being shunted into a siding at Langwith Junction shed on the day after Bonfire Night 1960. The fifty-six year old tank arrived at Langwith in January 1960 after being rejected in turn by Barrow Hill and Mexborough. No.68623 was no stranger to foreign climes having spent most of the LNER year working from sheds in Scotland. In 1951 it moved south as far as Doncaster but they moved it on to Norwich who sent it onto the M&GN within months of arrival. Closure of that system released the 0-6-0T and it was sent to Staveley but not to the ex-GC shed where other ex-GER six-coupled tanks resided; it went instead to the former Midland roundhouse at Barrow Hill which is where we came in. It was condemned in February 1961 and went back to Doncaster where it was processed through the new scrapping ground at the works. *David Dalton.*

For its size the city of Lincoln was well endowed with engine sheds, four of them in fact existed at Grouping but subsequent rationalisation of facilities by the LNER shortly after that event saw the former Great Eastern establishment at Pyewipe Junction closed. In 1939 the ex-Great Central shed on the east side of the city was also closed although the years of international conflict which followed saw its facilities in use until at least 1946. The next shed was the Great Northern depot situated west of the LNER passenger station. This particular establishment had been chosen by the LNER as their main facility in Lincoln and over the years either side of WW2 a large investment was made installing mechanical coaling plant, new turntable, and rebuilding the shed to last until closure in October 1964. That leaves just one more shed, the ex Midland Railway shed at St Marks dating from 1867. That place, along with its passenger station, goods facilities and dedicated route from the parent system in the west, was able to survive the upheavals thrust upon the LNER sheds and in about 1944 the LMS rebuilt the small two-road building to last for a couple more decades. This is the rear aspect of the shed in October 1954 with, ironically perhaps, two 'Directors' stabled. The ex-GC 4-4-0s were, at this period of their lives, working the Lincoln (St Marks)–Derby (Midland) passenger services over the former Midland route via Nottingham and Trent. To add another twist of irony, a handful of ex-GER D16 4-4-0s began the next class to be employed on those same services. St Marks station roof is visible above the wagons on the left. The engine shed finally closed in January 1959. *K.R.Pirt.*

Louth shed on Sunday 10th October 1954 with C12 No.67383 and J11 No.64307 on the turntable road. A two road shed had been provided here in 1848 by the East Lincolnshire Railway. Like all new railway ventures of that period, great things were also expected of the ELR but for the next hundred or so years it remained pretty much the same as it had on opening day! The shed adjoined the Up (east) side station buildings and remained unchanged until closure in 1956, excepting alteration to the original brick arch entrances courtesy of the Luftwaffe in 1941. Seasonal traffic saw the allocation vary in numbers throughout the sheds' life from sixteen or so engines to eight during times of recession, but the types remained a mixture of former Great Central and Great Northern types right up to closure in December 1956. Since Grouping two favourite types were as illustrated here but joining them at various times were ex-GC 4-4-0s, GER 0-6-0Ts, A5 Pacific tanks and ex-GN 0-6-0s. Having said that, the J11 seen here is a visitor from Immingham whilst the C12 was a local engine with but two months of life in front of it. *K.R.Pirt.*

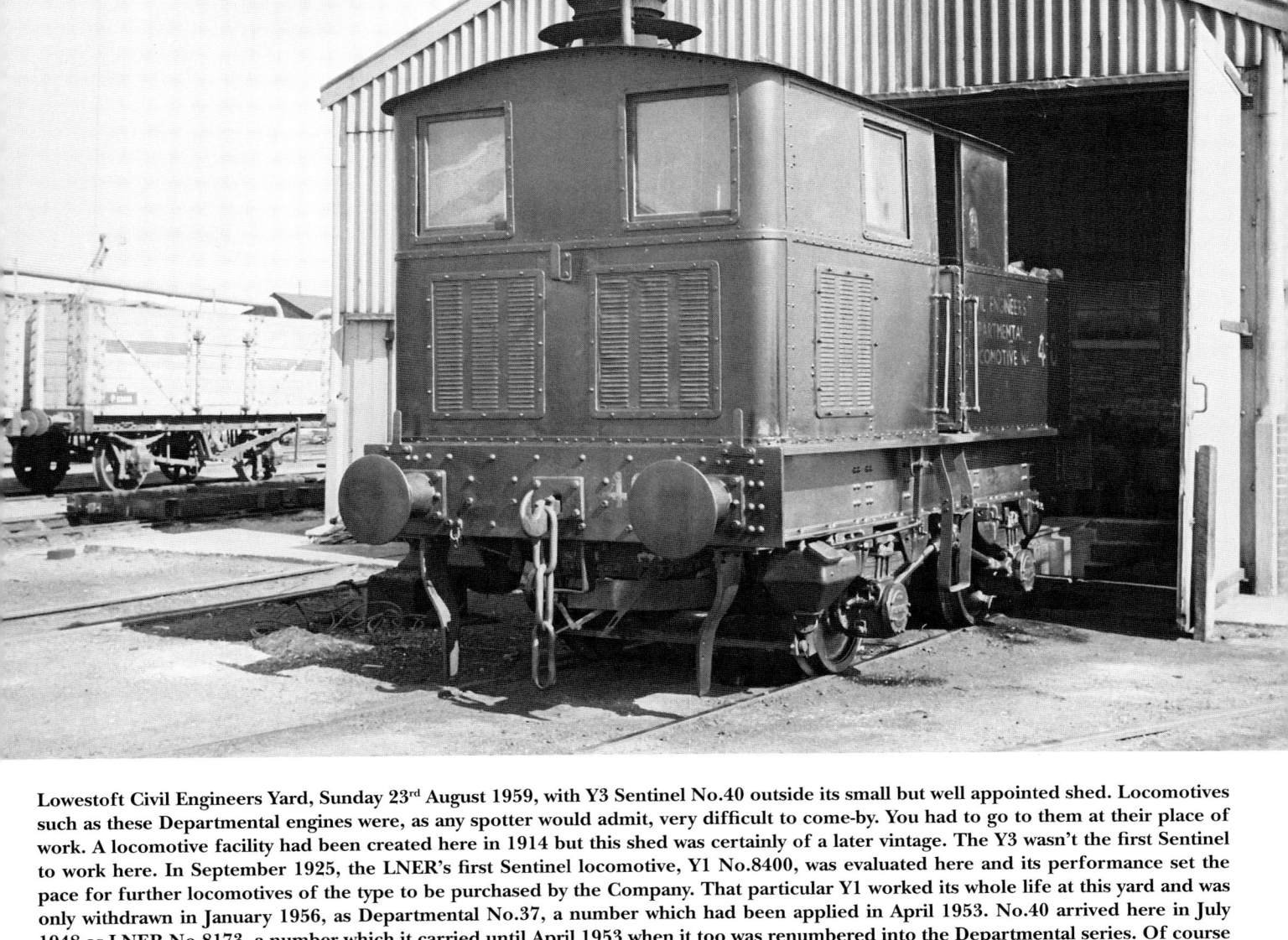

Lowestoft Civil Engineers Yard, Sunday 23rd August 1959, with Y3 Sentinel No.40 outside its small but well appointed shed. Locomotives such as these Departmental engines were, as any spotter would admit, very difficult to come-by. You had to go to them at their place of work. A locomotive facility had been created here in 1914 but this shed was certainly of a later vintage. The Y3 wasn't the first Sentinel to work here. In September 1925, the LNER's first Sentinel locomotive, Y1 No.8400, was evaluated here and its performance set the pace for further locomotives of the type to be purchased by the Company. That particular Y1 worked its whole life at this yard and was only withdrawn in January 1956, as Departmental No.37, a number which had been applied in April 1953. No.40 arrived here in July 1948 as LNER No.8173, a number which it carried until April 1953 when it too was renumbered into the Departmental series. Of course other Sentinels had worked here; Y1 No.8401 kept 8400 company from December 1926 until April 1951 when it moved to Norwich, and later Cambridge. Y3 No.63 was the next transfer in when, during October 1940, it joined the other two residents having moved from Colchester. No.63's stay was short however because six months later it went to Norwich prior to moving on to Cambridge. Renumbered 8173 in June 1946, it returned to Lowestoft on 11th July 1948. Two other Y3s worked here too. No.96 (later LNER 8177) came in 1936 and worked the yard until condemned in March 1963 as Departmental 41. No.98 (LNER 8178) arrived in 1937 but left for Cambridge in July 1952. At the end of 1961 the Sentinel from Hall Hills in Boston (DPT. No.7), was drafted in to help the remaining two engines. It was a busy place with four locomotives at its beck and call. Our subject was condemned in May 1964; at the same time as the shed closed. No.7 was spare engine by then. *David Dalton.*

As mentioned on page 2, J17 No.65583 did appear to be in good condition. This three-quarter rear view, taken on that same Sunday at March shed – 16th March 1958 – shows the engine to be in excellent condition although the College of Heralds would have something to say about the wrong-handed BR crest! One of the reasons for the 0-6-0s external state lay in the fact that it had completed a General overhaul just seven weeks beforehand. *David Dalton.*

The intense sunlight of the latter part of winter can highlight much which might otherwise be murky but it can also intensify to the point of blinding the camera. Such was the case at March shed on 16th March 1958, when J15 No.65420 was acting as one of the depots snow plough engines. Flanked on the left by WD No.90028 and on the right by J19 No.64661, the 0-6-0 presents an unusual aspect rarely photographed and indeed rarely carried out at most depots during BR days – the method of securing the snow plough to the engine. Three substantial brackets bolted to the bufferbeam would be regarded as quite normal but the removal of the buffers in order to fit the device in place is somewhat different! Its winter duties were, perhaps, nearly completed but winter is near far away during the month of March so this particular 0-6-0 would probably remain in this state until mid April. In the meantime No.65420 would not be undertaking any serious shunting duties anywhere. *David Dalton.*

March shed, Sunday 26th June 1961, with three visitors stabled for the weekend: York based V2 No.60961, Stanier 8F No.48305, from Northampton and an unidentified BR Standard 9F. None of the latter class were allocated to March during this time, although when the Eastern Region started to receive the new 9F 2-10-0s in their midst, from April 1954, a number of the first batch were initially sent to March shed (92010-92014, 92043 and 92044) but those were all dispersed to other ER depots by mid-1957. However, they remained daily visitors. *David Dalton.*

No stranger to March shed. B17/6 No.61626 had spent the initial ten years of BR allocated to March shed but a transfer in late November 1958 sent it off to King's Lynn for the winter. On its return to 31B in April 1959 it had received little in the way of cleaning during its winter sojourn by the sea. A transfer to Cambridge in December 1959 to replace a condemned B2 was short-lived because. Due a boiler change, No.61626 was sent off to Doncaster but on entering that works it too was condemned on 11th January 1960. It was no surprise that the 4-6-0 would not receive a major overhaul, its sister engines had been falling victim during the past couple of years and with the last of the B2s gone, it was time to clear up the stragglers of B17 class. Note the BR built 350 h.p. 0-6-0 diesel-electric shunter on the right. March had looked after the first LNER built examples in the post-war period with some success and it received just one new batch when D3491 to D3494 were allocated during April and May 1958, from the BR workshop at Darlington. Thereafter no more new diesel shunters ever came to the place; a few were eventually drafted in from other depots but only to replace those from the initial batch which had been transferred. Those four remained the only new, 'straight out of the box' shunters they ever got at March in BR days! Forming the right background to the picture is the south-west corner of the GER-built engine shed, complete with water tank, which was opened in 1884. *K.R.Pirt.*

Between the sheds at March in April 1960 a lone and extremely filthy 'Austerity' No.90428, makes a stark contrast to the haze around the 'wash-out' shed some distance away. Besides the depots at Colwick, Mexborough and Wakefield, this East Anglian depot could also boast to having a large allocation of the WD 2-8-0s throughout the BR period, and indeed in latter LNER days too. No.90428 was one of those purchased by the LNER, a move which set a precedence for BR. Behind the engine can be seen the 'Cenotaph' type coaling plant which, in this rather flat landscape, could be seen for miles around. *D.H.Beecroft.*

March depot, May 1964 with B1 No.61181, now masquerading as Departmental Loco. No.18, alongside the 'wash-out' shed. This engine had transferred to March from Darnall in January 1963 and after being withdrawn on 25th November of the same year, it was designated to be a Stationary Boiler, apparently for the shed in the background, a duty which it undertook until late in 1965 when it was condemned and sold for scrap. A total of seventeen B1s became Departmental engines from November 1963 onwards although No.61323 was condemned virtually straight away and was not renumbered (24). However, the last ones held their own until April 1968. Note the similarity of the shed design to that at Cambridge. *David Dalton.*

The north side of Mexborough shed yard on Sunday 17th July 1955, with O4 No.63673 heading a line of classmates. Considering that this depot had a substantial number of WD 2-8-0s allocated throughout all of the BR period, usually outnumbering the resident O4s by about 2 to 1, there are only three or so identifiable in this view as against a dozen or so of the Robinson designed engines. Of course, throughout the 1950s Mexborough's allocation of 2-8-0 freight locomotives changed considerably because at the start of the decade 36B, its BR code to 1958, housed not only former GC and 'Austerity' types, it had more than a dozen of the Gresley O2 class too. However, these later moved back to depots in the old Great Northern territory such as Colwick, although a number went to Frodingham, whilst O4s from those sheds took their place. Regarding the WD 2-8-0s, Mexborough could always boast to having a concentration of at least fifty of the class allocated virtually up to closure. Note that all the tenders are topped-up ready for Monday's start of another week of graft. All the coaling was of course carried out at the shed's manual coal stage, a colossal effort being required from the coalmen to keep this fleet satisfied. Even the depot's breakdown crane was employed regularly to shift the average daily requirement of 220 tons. It was not until 1961 that a mechanical coaling plant was built at this place and then only because the manual stage had become utterly unsafe. As far back as 1936 a mechanical apparatus had been planned but various outside influences had got in the way over the intervening years. To add insult, the depot closed in 1964 and the coaling plant was demolished just a year afterwards. *David Dalton.*

A long-time resident of Mexborough was Thompson B1 No.61167 which is stabled on the coaling stage road along with a sister engine and a WD 2-8-0 on Sunday 17th July 1955. The proximity of the turntable is readily apparent from this view. In the background, one of the depot's handful of J11 0-6-0s, No.64356, buffers up to another 'Austerity'. With the opening of the Manchester-Sheffield-Wath electrification in 1954, Mexborough's steam locomotive allocation fell somewhat by about a quarter to less than a hundred engines. However, the opening of the new purpose built depot for the MSW electric locomotives at Wath-upon-Dearne took quite a number of footplate staff away from 36B, putting them to work from the electric depot, which became a sub shed of Mexborough. That event was yet another reason for the delay in providing mechanical coaling facilities at Mexborough. *David Dalton.*

A quiet New England engine shed on Saturday 27th March 1965, with A3 No.60112 and an unidentified B1 standing beneath the water gantry in the south yard. The depot had closed to steam some two months earlier and these two cold and derelict hulks were waiting for a tow to their respective scrapyards; the Pacific went to Norwich probably with the B1 attached. It will be seen that all the valve gear except the connecting rod is still in place on both locomotives, the latter being secured to the respective running plates with rope; the B1 has two lengths of rope in use whereas the A3s situation appears somewhat precarious especially if towed away in that condition. Note also that the 34E shed plate is still fixed to the smokebox door. The blackened building to the right was the old fitting shop which dated from the days when New England played a bigger role in the GNR's locomotive overhaul business. Since then, the shop had undertaken less demanding work but nevertheless remained open to the end of steam at the shed sorting out the depot's more awkward and exacting running repairs. The shed road on which these locomotives are standing was one of nine covered by the through shed in the left background. In 1967 this particular shed building was used to house the redundant goods vehicles of the defunct Roadrailer experiment which was never pursued with any real commitment by BR. *David Dalton.*

New England shed, April 1960, with Ivatt Cl.4 No.43151 at the eastern point of the triangle whilst undertaking a turning manoeuvre. The buildings behind the tender are the old locomotive workshops from GNR days but which remained in use for running repairs until the closure of New England. Access to the shops could be gained via a traverser set into the layout of the south-east wall of the building. To the right was the coaling plant and coaling stage, with access to the north-west yard of the engine shed. This 'Mogul' had just been transferred to New England from Colwick and it was to remain here for three years before moving on to Barrow Hill, and then Crewe South in October 1964. Elsewhere in this album, there is an illustration of two of these Cl.4s as turned out new from Doncaster 'Plant' works in 1951. No.43151 wasn't one of them but it did start life in the same condition when it commenced work from Melton Constable, on the former M&GNJR., in November 1951. When that system closed the 2-6-0 was sent to Stratford for a year! *D.H.Beecroft.*

After three years working on the London, Tilbury & Southend line, allocated to Plaistow shed, J17s Nos.65588, with 65533 behind, are stabled on a siding at 33A on 27th May 1955 waiting for haulage to Stratford and return to the GE Lines. These two, along with three other J17s, had arrived on the LT&S line in early 1952 and were all fitted with Hudd ATC before they could go to work. The pair had completed their stint now and, after having the ATC removed, they have been set aside on this siding; it once led to the turntable behind the photographer but had been dead-ended at some time in the past. Note the chalked instruction DONT MOVE, and the 33A shedplates still in situ. *David Dalton.*

Just out of Doncaster 'Plant' works, after a General overhaul, Peppercorn K1 No.62054 looks out of place at Retford Thrumpton shed on Sunday 10th June 1962. It would be safe to say that the 2-6-0 was probably the cleanest locomotive on shed that day given the general state of the rest of the allocation at 36E. Retford's 2-8-0 allocation was, at that time, going through a state of flux with the O2s being withdrawn and replaced in the main by WD 2-8-0s which were to remain at the Nottinghamshire depot until closure in January 1965. This K1, a fairly recent addition to Retford's stud, arrived in October 1961 from March and would work until the end of December 1964. *K.R.Pirt.*

Retford Thrumpton, the former GCR shed on Friday evening, 4th April 1958 with O4 No.63608 stabled for the weekend. One of the original GC built and operated 2-8-0s, this engine had been renumbered from No.3511 in February 1947 to take up the number vacated by O4 No.5383 which was sent out to the Middle East on war service in September 1941. No.5383, which became WD 711 never returned to the UK so, in order to close up gaps in the 1946 LNER renumbering scheme, and release 35XX numbers for LNER operated Stanier 2-8-0s, many of those early number O4s i.e. 3500 to 3569, were renumbered to fill the gaps left by those engines which had left the country. Our subject here was soon to visit the works at Gorton for a much needed General overhaul and to receive a reconditioned boiler which would see it through to withdrawal in May 1961. However, the Gorton visit was still two months away and No.63608 had a lot of work to do during that time, starting on Monday next. Note the sheerlegs, a typical GC design, which initially were hand operated but in latter years, at some depots, were connected to electric motors or fuel driven generators - those fitters certainly had it easy in BR days! The terraced property on London Road the old A1, look over this, the east end of the shed yard. *K.R.Pirt.*

Yes, its 'Flaming June' in 1965 and we are at the former, albeit rebuilt by BR, Great Northern Railway engine shed at Retford. On the left is the new order in the shape of a BR built 350 h.p. 0-6-0 diesel-electric shunter, and, inside the shed, what appears to be a brand new Brush Type 4. The big diesel was probably there on crew training duties for the forthcoming MGR traffic which was to transform the locomotive workings in this part of the country. On the right is the old order represented by B1 No.61127 and the 15-ton steam breakdown crane stabled at the side of the shed. The shed at Thrumpton had closed at the beginning of the year and what remained of its steam allocation, after withdrawals and transfers, was sent here, amongst them twenty WD 2-8-0s, half a dozen O4s and eight B1s of which No.61127 was the last one left at the shed. In mid-June the 4-6-0 was sent to Doncaster so that Retford could be closed as a steam depot and be used temporarily as a stabling point for diesel locomotives. After less than a month, Doncaster sent No.61127 (note the external condition of the engine) to Frodingham shed but its services there were hardly required so that in July it was condemned and sold for scrap. Retford shed, or to be more precise, the shed at this particular site was eventually given up and later sold intact to a local enterprise. It is still standing in 2011 and serving a useful purpose in private ownership. *David Dalton.*

Saffron Walden, Sunday 25th September 1955 with E4 No.62792 stabled for the weekend. A recent transfer from Norwich had brought this ancient 2-4-0 to end its days at Cambridge, the latter shed of course supplying Saffron Walden with motive power. The tiny one-road shed is just out of frame to the left although the adjacent water tank is just visible, the track leading to the shed and the 40ft turntable behind, disappear behind the growing ash and clinker pile. The exact duty of the E4 at this place is unknown but pick-up goods on the line were usually in the hands of tender engines. Externally No.62792 did not appear too healthy but it was not withdrawn until June 1956. *David Dalton.*

A little bit further along the yard at Saffron Walden on that Sunday in September 1955 was this 0-4-4T. A stranger in town? This former North Eastern tank, certainly wasn't a stranger in these parts! Push-pull fitted G5 No.67322 had been resident at Cambridge since July 1951 when it had transferred from Stratford after a thirteen year stint working the Seven Sisters-Palace Gates service. Two other members of G5 class, which had also been at Stratford working similar duties on the Epping-Ongar section besides the Palace gates job, had joined No.67322 at Cambridge in 1951 so that the trio could work the Audley End-Bartlow passenger trains. For this duty they were stabled at Saffron Walden which was a sub shed of Cambridge. Although fitted with the push-pull gear at Stratford works in 1939, the G5s still made the long trek to Darlington for any scheduled repairs. Finally, as they were withdrawn, the G5 returned to their native heath; No.67322 was condemned on 1st November 1956. Meanwhile, the shed at Saffron Walden continued to house the motive power used on the Audley End service and was eventually closed in July 1958. It is not recorded if any engine was actually inside the shed on this particular Sunday. *K.R.Pirt.*

An undated but BR period view of Southend Victoria engine shed. This former GER shed consisted a two-road through type building situated just north of Southend (Victoria) station, on the east side of the line. We are looking at its north end with three N7s stabled outside. The mineral wagon with its, propped, open door, suggests that coaling was being carried out by hand from the wagon whereas Victoria shed was blessed initially with a coal stage from opening in 1889. Later, BR built a mechanical coaling plant. This view must date from the period when the coaling plant was either being erected or it was out of action. This small yet busy shed was closed as electrification reached Southend in 1957. *David Dalton.*

South Lynn engine shed, 8th May 1954. This four-road, dead-ended shed consisted two wooden buildings, the first two-road section of which was opened in January 1886. The virtually identical structure alongside was provided at a later date to serve the growing fleet of Midland & Great Northern engines. At nationalisation, having had no investment during the intervening years, the shed was becoming quite dilapidated but it remained serviceable, albeit with chunks missing, until BR decided to replace it in 1957. *K.R.Pirt.*

The rebuilt engine shed at South Lynn. The four-road footprint was kept but everything else was swept away. A building consisting of a steel frame, clad in corrugated materials on brick foundations was erected in 1958 ready for closure less than one year later. The cost of the new build must have been an accountants dream whereby it could be added to the annual costs of keeping the M&GN open! However, witness the scene above which was captured on film on Sunday 16th October 1960! Although the shed did play host to stored locomotives from the closed depot at nearby King's Lynn, most of those in the picture were in steam. J17 No.65576 on the right was a March engine at this time and was certainly active until the summer of 1962. Eventually, when the railway did give up the site, the shed became a depot for National Carriers Limited – NCL. *David Dalton.*

(above) Stratford shed, 16th October 1955. Hatfield based N7/5 No.69635 is just out of shops after its final General overhaul. *(below)* Same day at Stratford shed in 1955. Stratford based N7 No.69624 – apparently – was soon to enter shops for alteration to N7 Part 5 and its last 'General' – Compare with above! *both K.R.Pirt.*

Stratford shed, 16th October 1955 with one of the depot's army of 0-6-0 tank engines, J68 No.68655. This was one of the ten shunting types found within class J68. Three-link as opposed to screw coupling was provided, unbalanced wheels were fitted and just a steam brake for the engine. Because condensing apparatus was not fitted, the side tanks had flat tops. No.68655 had just completed a General overhaul (15th August to 17th September) at the nearby works hence the semi clean appearance. *K.R.Pirt.*

Wisbech shed on Sunday 6th April 1952 with one of the distinctive Wisbech & Upwell J70 tram engines hiding in the shed whilst a more conventional 0-6-0T stables outside. The first thing of notice is the cleanliness of the yard. Next is the lamp-post (still gas fitted) fabricated from rail! This place was established as an engine shed for the W&UT in 1883. At first a single road shed – the left side in the illustration – was provided but twelve years later a virtually identical shed with a slightly higher roof was attached to the north – right side – wall in order to house the growing locomotive stud. The first engines shedded here were three new 0-4-0 tram engines (LNER Class Y6), which were followed in 1892 by three more new Y6 class. In 1908 one of the new and larger six-coupled tram engines (LNER Class J70) arrived to complement the six smaller engines. By Grouping the allocation at Wisbech comprised six Y6, Nos.0125, 0126, 0129, 132, 133, 134, along with J70 No.136. All but one of the Y6 which survived to Grouping ended their days at Wisbech, the odd man out being No.134 (68083) which was the last of them but had transferred to March in July 1952 – replaced by a diesel shunter – only to be withdrawn four months later. J70 engines arrived at various times during LNER days to replace withdrawn Y6 and by Nationalisation the allocation consisted three J70: Nos.8217, 8222, 8223 and the two surviving Y6: Nos.8082 and 8083. Dieselisation took hold on the W&UT by 1955 and the shed lost some of its charm when the newer section was demolished. It finally closed in May 1966. *David Dalton.*

The north-west corner of Woodford shed on Tuesday 21st July 1964 with five very different locomotives in view. Nearest is derelict J39 No.64747, with an unidentified Stanier 8F behind. Beneath the sheerlegs V2 No.60810 appears to be stabling rather than receiving any sort of remedial attention, whilst further along the road a 9F and a 'Royal Scot', the latter no doubt one of Annesley's charges, have faint traces of steam around them. Our J39, note the numberplate still in situ, had just finished duties as the shed's Stationary Boiler, a task it had performed since being withdrawn in November 1962. By Christmas a Sheffield merchant would have purchased the 0-6-0 for scrap. After a lifetime of working from depots located along the length and breadth of the GC route; another journey over its metals was in the offing but this time it was to be one-way only as far as Killamarsh. *David Dalton.*

Although part of the London Midland regime when this scene was captured on film in 1965, Woodford shed had its origins deeply embedded in the Eastern Region. Opened by the Great Central in 1897 as part of the London Extension works, Woodford Halse was concerned with the movement of freight not only to the capital but also to locations in the Western Region on which it bordered. During WW2 it became an important motive power changeover point for trains carrying war materials to the south coast ports from manufacturing areas in the north of the country. The place was also famous for being the southern concentration point of the so-called 'Annesley Runners' which, during BR days especially, saw loaded coal trains from Annesley yards hauled at fast speeds to Woodford for further distribution to points south. The locomotives involved were usually those from Annesley shed, Thompson O1s, and latterly BR Standard 9F 2-10-0s which would arrive at Woodford, service on shed and work back to Nottinghamshire same day with the same crew. The round trip was approximately seven hours so that one 9F could do two round trips every 24-hours, of course with two sets of men. All that was to change when the LMR took over the former GCR route in 1958, with a view to closing down not only the coal traffic but the whole route too. It took the LM authorities a number of years to achieve their goal but by 1965 it was virtually completed. One of the first objectives was to change the ex-LNER motive power to a mixture of former LMS locomotives and BR Standards. The same exercise was being carried out at Annesley and Colwick where some perfectly able, and in some cases ex works, locomotives were sent for scrap in what can only be described as wanton vandalism and a disgraceful waste of public money. In June 1965 Woodford Halse was closed, its parent system following close behind. *F.W. & C. Dunne.*

Yarmouth Vauxhall, 27th March 1955. With the engine shed in the background, two of the depots residents, F6 No.67235 and D16/3 No.62604 are out-on-a-limb on a siding in the south-west corner of the depot. For its size, Yarmouth was well blessed with engine sheds, three in total, all surviving into BR days. Two of the sheds, South Town and Vauxhall were built by the Great Eastern whilst the third, and last to be erected, was Beach which was owned by the M&GN. All three sheds supplied motive power for the passenger stations with the same names. Vauxhall shed was built in 1883 and replaced an earlier establishment of Yarmouth & Norwich Railway origin, dating from 1844 and which was demolished to allow enlargement of the Vauxhall passenger station. Of our two engines, the F6 had transferred into Vauxhall shed in September 1953 from Yarmouth Beach where it had gone in December 1947 after thirty-six years at Stratford. For use on the M&GN section it had been fitted with tablet exchange apparatus but that had been removed when re-allocated to Vauxhall. The 2-4-2T didn't have much longer for this world and was condemned in January 1956. The 4-4-0 was a bit more fortunate, at least in the short term. The same age as the tank engine, it had been subject to two re-buildings during its life. Arriving in Yarmouth during the darkest days of WW2, it resided at the resort town – shared by South Town and Vauxhall sheds – until the closure of the former depot in November 1959; Vauxhall had closed in the previous January. Lowestoft was the D16's next shed (it had actually spent three weeks there in October 1945) but with the diesel fleet on the GE lines growing weekly, there was no place for the 4-4-0 and it was condemned in February 1960. *David Dalton.*